PADUCAH

Portrait of a River Town
by Richard Holland

CHIEF
PADUKE
FOR WHOM
GEN WILLIAM CLARK
NAMED PADUCAH

"Delta Queen" on the Ohio River
Paducah, Kentucky

CONTENTS

First National Bank.
Paducah. Ky.

HIGH SCHOOL, PADUCAH, KY.

Paducah High School (later Washington Junior High) in the 1200 block of Broadway (now demolished).

INTRODUCTION

This book is the fortuitous result of two unusual interests. The first is my own study of the history and development of Paducah and my efforts to learn more about the significant people and events in our town's past. The second is Bill Schroeder's avid pursuit of historic postcards of Paducah — photographic souvenirs of our town and its buildings. We have combined these two interests to provide a portrait of our town's past.

The research resources for studying our town's history are wonderful. In my research efforts, I have used such resources as city directories, Chamber of Commerce scrapbooks, newspaper clippings, local promotional brochures, property deeds and records, city ordinance books, old maps, magazine articles, as well as the many excellent history books written on Paducah. We have been fortunate to have had historians like Fred Neuman, Hall Allen, John Robertson, Richard Fairhurst and Camille Wells to research and interpret our town's past.

But nothing is more fun or informative for an historian to study than an old photograph or postcard. The information that these can provide is limitless — what buildings looked like, what kind of clothes people wore, what stores and businesses were in operation, how areas like the riverfront or the market house originally appeared, what forms of transportation were being used, how the town celebrated special events and holidays. Plus, the backs of postcards contain personal messages written by one person to another — a reminder that real people once lived and breathed in the world illustrated by the postcards.

This book is a "portrait" of a river town that we know as Paducah. Like any good portrait, it should contain enough information to be an accurate portrayal of the subject. But it can also be even more. By reading the text and studying the illustrations, the reader should also be able to discover new information and themes. That's the joy of history. Hopefully, it will serve as a helpful resource for future historians studying the development of our town.

Richard Holland

1825–1850

Paducah has always been a town oriented to the river. The first settlers set up a primitive community at the juncture of the Ohio and Tennessee rivers. By 1827, the settlement, known as Pekin, contained a few houses and a dry goods store. William Clark, who held title to thousands of acres of land in the Jackson Purchase, commissioned the first plat for the town. Under Clark's direction, the first streets and blocks were laid out and lots surveyed so that they could be sold to new settlers. An area for future public use was set aside by Clark and by 1836 it contained the county courthouse and the town's market house.

Clark also changed the name of the community to Paducah, reflecting the area's Indian heritage. Paducah was officially incorporated as a town by an act of the Kentucky State Legislature on January 11, 1830. A town government was formed in 1831 and at its first meeting the board of trustees dealt with issues connected to streets and the riverfront.

Efforts to bring enlightenment to the community followed. In 1836, a lottery was held to raise money for two educational academies. The Methodist denomination organized the first church in Paducah in 1833 and this was soon followed by Baptist, Catholic, Presbyterian, and Episcopal denominations.

Paducah's location on the Ohio river and its close proximity to three other major rivers were the reasons for the town's early growth. Paducah could claim to have direct access to more miles of navigable water than any other town in the country. This advantage, plus the town's year-round open harbor, allowed Paducah to rightfully claim the title of "River City."

Market Building–Paducah, Ky.

PLATTING THE TOWN

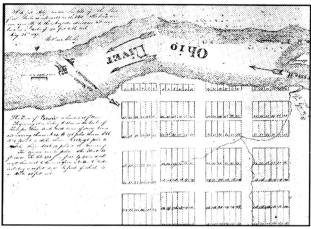

The original plat for the town of Paducah was drawn on May 26, 1829. This event was one of many in Paducah's early history that was connected to two members of the Clark family, George Rogers and William.

In 1795, General George Rogers Clark was rewarded for his military

William Clark's original plat for Paducah, now displayed in the Market House Museum.

service in the Revolutionary War with two tracts of land in southwestern Kentucky totaling 73,962 acres. One tract of 37,000 acres included the present site of Paducah, which was then only a primitive settlement called Pekin. After George Rogers Clark's death in 1818, this land passed to William Clark, his younger brother.

In order to encourage the development of a community at the confluence of the Ohio and Tennessee rivers, William Clark authorized the platting of a town. It was through this plat that the original streets, blocks and lot lines of Paducah were laid out. The initial town plan was composed of 12 blocks containing 12 lots each. Each lot had 57.5 feet of frontage and 173 feet in depth. Twenty-four smaller lots were laid out along the steep riverfront.

William Clark came from St. Louis to his new town and remained here for two weeks while the surveying took place. When finished, the new town plat was recorded in McCracken County Deed Book A by county surveyor Jonathan Martin. The original plat describes the town boundary as starting at a hickory tree and stone located on the bank of the Tennessee River.

William Clark began to immediately sell lots to early settlers in Paducah. The lot at the northeast corner of First and Broadway was sold for $12. Other lots sold for $10. Land at the outskirts of town sold for 10 to 25 cents per acre. Clark set aside an area on South Market Street (now Second Street) for public purposes. The first McCracken County Courthouse in Paducah was built on this land in 1831, and the first Market House in 1836. Because of his donation of these lots to the town, Clark was exempted from taxation on his property by the town trustees.

FIRST TOWN GOVERNMENT

City Hall, Paducah, Ky.

The Paducah City Government has its origins on May 5, 1831 when the Chairman and Board of Trustees of Paducah held their first meeting. An election for the Board of Trustees had taken place three days earlier at the home of George Dunn. At this meeting F. A. Harrison was elected chairman and Dunn, Dr. Robert Fletcher, Robert Enders, and Thomas Flournoy were elected as trustees.

The first city offices appointed by the board were Clerk and Assessor, Collector, and Overseer of Streets, reflecting the board's early priorities of collecting taxes and maintaining streets. One of the first pieces of business of the board was to pass ordinances requiring people to remove their fences and houses from the street and to forbid keelboats from landing at the riverfront directly in front of town.

The minutes for the first meeting also noted that General William Clark had given the town several lots and therefore was exempted from paying taxes. These lots would later have a market house and a courthouse built on them.

The total value of taxable property in Paducah in 1831 was $29,270. Taxes of 18.75 cents per 100 dollars were levied, with a total amount of $45.50 to be collected for the year.

FIRSTS FOR PADUCAH

A series of "firsts" record Paducah's growth from a primitive settlement to a real community. Among these firsts are:

1811   First steamboat on the Ohio River, the "New Orleans," stops at the mouth of the Tennessee River on its voyage from Pittsburgh to New Orleans.

1821   A pioneer settlement is started by four families and the first houses are constructed.

1822   First ferry service to Illinois is started by Valentine Owen.

1826   First commercial store is built on the riverfront and serves as a trading post for hunters and river travelers.

1827   The first plat for the town is drawn by William Clark's agent and the new town is named Paducah.

1828   The first inn, the Indian Queen, is built.

1829   The first private academy is opened.

1830   Paducah is incorporated as a town.

1834   First church congregation is organized by the Methodists.
        First newspaper, the weekly *Express*, is published.

1836   First Market House is built.
        First neighborhoods are incorporated into the town.

1837   First bank, the Exchange Bank of Paducah, is established.

1842   First improvements to the riverfront are made, including graveling the levee.

1847   First lumber mill and brick yard are opened by James Langstaff.

1853   First industry in Paducah, the Marine Railways, is opened.

1854   First black church is organized as the African Baptist Church (now the Washington Street Baptist Church).

1857   First railroad connection is made to Paducah.

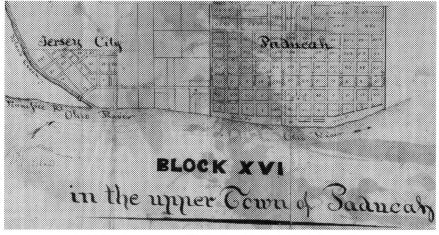

An 1847 watercolor map of Paducah and its first suburb, Jersey City.

CAPTAIN VALENTINE OWEN

Probably no person is more closely associated with Paducah's early history than Captain Valentine Owen. As an adventurous youth of nineteen, Valentine Owen paddled a canoe down the Ohio river to the primitive town of Pekin. In 1823, he set up the first ferry service from the town to Illinois, providing an important trade link for the town and creating the community's first river industry. His success allowed him to purchase large parcels of land, including the island at the mouth of the Tennessee River that is still known as Owen Island.

In 1830, he built the first two-story residence in Paducah and the following year married Elizabeth Walters. That year he also built the Rising Sun tavern. Because it was built on the riverside, the tavern had a three-story facade facing the Ohio River and a two-story facade facing First Street. The tavern was called the Rising Sun because it was the tallest building in town and the first to catch the morning sun. The name Rising Sun was painted in bold letters above the third floor windows, making it easily visible from the river.

Valentine Owen was also involved in the town's government and was named Overseer of Streets in 1831. This was an important position in a developing town. Owen was responsible for improving the conditions of the streets and removing obstructions like fences and houses from the public right-of-ways.

Valentine Owen and his family continued the ferry service to Illinois for many years. In 1850, he built the Transport, a sidewheel steamboat, to ferry passengers and cargo to and from Illinois. Valentine Owen died in 1874 and was buried in Oak Grove Cemetery. The family's last ferry, the Betty Owen, burned on February 5, 1912 and this Paducah tradition came to an end.

Paducah's Harbor—Paducah, Ky.

JOHN SLEETH AND THE
FIRST UNDERWATER CABLE

In 1845, Paducah became the site of the first successfully laid submarine telegraph cable in the world. In the early 1840's, the telegraph line at Paducah that connected St. Louis and Nashville ran across the Ohio River and was supported by large staffs erected on the Kentucky and Illinois shores and on an island in the river. Constant attention was needed to maintain the line and keep it high above the water level. In 1845, an employee of the telegraph company, Captain John Boyd Sleeth, invented a primitive way to insulate the telegraph lines with canvas that had been soaked in pine tar pitch. Sleeth then covered the telegraph line and canvas with coils to create a cable that could be laid underwater. A mile-long cable was made and laid on the bottom of the Ohio River from Paducah to the Illinois shore. When connected to the telegraph system, the cable worked well for several weeks.

Eventually the insulation became water-soaked and the submarine cable was abandoned. While Sleeth's system worked only a short time, it did prove that the idea was practicable provided a better insulation could be found. Sleeth's system attracted the attention of inventor Cyrus Field, who sent a representative to meet with Sleeth with the proposal to form a development partnership for the submarine cable system. Sleeth declined the offer and returned to being a riverboat captain. He never patented his concept or tried to resurrect the idea. Cyrus Field went on to develop Sleeth's concept and in 1848 a submarine telegraph cable was successfully laid from New York to Jersey City. Sleeth's invention was largely forgotten until 1897, when a section of the original cable was discovered on the shore of the Ohio River. The cable was rescued and eventually given to Sleeth's son. National recognition finally came when John Boyd Sleeth's invention of the submarine telegraph cable was recorded in the June 23, 1890 issue of *Scientific American*. Sleeth died in 1895 and was buried in Oak Grove Cemetery.

MOONLIGHT ON THE OHIO RIVER, SHOWING PADUCAH, KY.

Harper's Weekly *drawing of Paducah's Marine Hospital in 1862.*

MARINE HOSPITAL

The United States Marine Hospital in Paducah was one of four hospitals built by the federal government along the nation's inland waterways around 1850. The purpose of the marine hospitals was "to take care of those engaged in navigating the Ohio and the Mississippi Rivers who, owning to fatigue and exposure incident to long voyages, become sick and languish..."

The prototype of the marine hospital was designed by Robert Mills, who was appointed federal architect in 1836. Mills was the first native-born American to train specifically as an architect. As the official architect for the government, Mills was involved in every major federal project in the 1830s and 1840s. He was especially esteemed for the Egyptian obelisk he designed for the Washington Monument and the Greek Revival fireproof building he designed as the headquarters of the U. S. Treasury.

Mills continued designing federal buildings until 1851. His prototype design for the inland marine hospitals was carried out by Stephen Long, who modified Mill's design somewhat. The Paducah Marine Hospital was a four-story structure with advanced square pavilions at the corners, recessed open galleries on the north and south sides, and an octagonal cupola that admitted light into the interior. The construction of the Marine Hospital was supervised by George Davis, who came to Paducah in 1949 and remained one of the town's leading architects until his death around 1893.

During the Civil War, the Marine Hospital was taken over by federal soldiers after the occupation of Paducah in 1861 and was used for the storage of ammunition. Fort Anderson was built adjoining the hospital, which burned around 1862. A drawing of the Marine Hospital in Paducah appeared in an issue of *Harper's Weekly* that profiled Paducah under the Northern occupation.

PADUCAH, KY.

PADUCAH WHARF AND CONFLUENCE OF
OHIO AND TENNESSEE RIVERS

1851–1870

Paducah enjoyed a period of remarkable growth between 1830 and 1850 and by 1851 had a population of 2,428 people. The growth of the population was matched by an expansion of the town limits, which grew to 96 blocks by 1856.

Much of this population growth was due to mass immigration of Germans escaping harsh conditions in Europe and starting new lives in Ohio River towns. Many of these immigrants were Jewish merchants who built a substantial commercial district on Market Street and along Broadway.

Besides being a regional retail and service center, Paducah developed as an important transportation center for mid-America. Actions by the town's government led to important economic development projects, including the construction of the Paducah Marine Ways in 1854 and the connection of Paducah to the nation's railway systems in 1857. Paducah's continued growth and prosperity were guaranteed by the links to the rivers and the railroads.

Paducah's status as an "up-and-coming" community was confirmed in 1856 when a new charter of incorporation was prepared by local attorney Quintus Q. Quigley and the Kentucky legislature confirmed Paducah as a third-class city.

Paducah's critical position at the heart of America's inland network of navigable waterways made the town an early target when the Civil War broke out. In one of the first actions in the western campaign to gain control of the Mississippi River, General Ulysses S. Grant and 5,000 Union soldiers occupied Paducah on September 23, 1861. From that point Paducah served as an important supply point for Union armies fighting in Tennessee and Georgia. Many of the town's structures were converted into housing for Union soldiers or into hospital facilities for wounded soldiers. Paducah's own brush with real fighting was the brief but intense Battle of Paducah, which took place on March 25, 1864.

PADUCAH'S CONNECTION
TO THE RAILROADS

On March 1, 1853, the Board of Trustees passed an ordinance stating that stock in the New Orleans and Ohio River railroad company in the amount of up to $200,000 would be subscribed to in the name of the Town of Paducah. This stock subscription was to help fund the construction of a rail line connecting Paducah to lines in Tennessee. The stock subscription was to be paid by 30 year bonds with a 6% interest rate. Local taxes were to be levied until the stock dividends would be able to cover the interest payments.

The citizens of Paducah went to the polls on June 29th to vote on the ordinance. A majority approved it. Taxes of $1.40 per $100 of property were levied to cover the interest on the bonds.

The construction of the railway line brought Lloyd Tilghman to Paducah. A graduate of West Point and a civil engineer, Tilghman supervised the surveying of the right-of-way and the actual construction of the railway. The first train pulled out of Paducah on July 4, 1854 for the seven mile trip to Florence, Kentucky. The locomotive pulling the train had been brought to Paducah by riverboat. Crowds gathered along the route to view this locomotive, which was capable of traveling at fifteen miles per hour.

Bad economic times slowed down the construction work and the railroad line did not connect to others in Tennessee until 1860. But from that moment on, Paducah's history was connected to the nation's railroads.

PADUCAH AND GULF RAILROAD.
Two Trains Leave Paducah Daily
FOR

UNION CITY, JACKSON AND ALL INTERMEDIATE POINTS.

Passengers desiring to go to New Orleans can go by Rail from Paducah via Jackson, Tennessee. Omnibusses and Carriages always on hand to convey passengers to and the Hotels or any part of the city.

LINN BOYD

Although he is almost forgotten today, Linn Boyd was a giant in both his size and in his prominence in state and national politics in the middle of the nineteenth century.

Boyd was born in Nashville, Tennessee, in 1800. As a young man, he worked with Andrew Jackson as a commissioner of the United States dealing with the Chickasaw Indians to acquire their lands south of the Ohio River. After becoming a resident of southwestern Kentucky, Boyd was elected to the state legislature. At 6 feet 4 inches and 220 pounds, Boyd towered over his fellow men. He was elected to the U. S. Congress in 1835, where he served with great distinction for 20 years. He worked with Henry Clay to create the Compromise of 1850, which helped to ease North-South tensions for a decade. He ranked with Clay and John Calhoun in popularity and leadership skills and followed Calhoun as speaker of the house in 1851.

After serving two terms as speaker of the house, Boyd retired to his home in Paducah, where he had moved in 1835. Despite his retirement, Boyd was promoted as a candidate for president of the United States in 1856 and came within 3 votes of being nominated by the Democratic party. He was elected lieutenant governor of Kentucky in 1859 but died before he could begin serving. He is buried in Paducah's Oak Grove Cemetery.

Oaklands, Linn Boyd's home that was located on Kentucky Avenue (now demolished).

MARINE RAILWAYS SYSTEM

On April 15, 1853, the Paducah Board of Trustees approved a contract with E. Murray & Co. of St. Louis to build a new marine railways system at the riverfront. The facility had the capacity to remove steamboats and other vessels from the water for repair work and to launch new crafts built in Paducah boat yards.

The patented system by Elijah Murray had the capacity to lift boats measuring up to 350 feet long out of the river. The system worked by maneuvering boats onto a series of wheeled cradles that ran on eight sections of inclined tracks. The tracks ran from below the river's edge to halfway up the river bank. The boats were floated over the submerged cradles and lifted out of the water and up the bank as the cradles moved up the inclined tracks. Steel cables attached to huge windlasses pulled the cradles upward. These windlasses were turned by a powerful steam engine.

The Paducah Marine Railways system was completed in March of 1864 and leased to the local Watts & Givens Company.

The construction of the Paducah Marine Railways led to the development of dry docks and boat-building facilities along the riverfront. Paducah has been a hub for the river industry ever since. The Paducah Marine Ways (as the operation was later known) continued in operation until the 1980s and the history of the company closely reflected the entire history of Paducah.

Paducah Marine Ways at the turn of the century.

MCCRACKEN COUNTY COURTHOUSE — 1857

By the 1850s, local citizens who realized that the courthouse on Market Street was not large enough to serve the county's needs took steps to build a larger one. In 1857, the county government purchased a block of land to the southwest of downtown Paducah for the construction of the new courthouse. The courthouse was constructed by Louisville builder John F. Hendren for $27,830. Some local citizens objected to the courthouse being built away from the then downtown area but the county proceeded with the project.

The 1857 McCracken County Courthouse was one of the first monumental buildings in Paducah. The two-story, brick building had round-arched windows and a central cupola. Projecting gables topped with pediments contained the entrances to the building. The corners of the building were delineated with raised quoins. Located on the grounds of the courthouse were a cast-iron fountain and two pairs of tin Civil War soldier statues that marked the sidewalks leading up to the entrances. The courthouse remained standing until it was replaced by the current McCracken County Courthouse in the early 1940s.

An exciting day in the history of the 1857 McCracken County Courthouse was June 13, 1909, when William Jennings Bryan spoke on the courthouse steps. Bryan was one of the most popular men in America at the turn of the century and was a candidate for President in 1896, 1900, and 1908. He would later play a prominent part in the John T. Scopes trial in Dayton, Tennessee. Scopes, who was placed on trial for teaching about the theory of evolution, was a native of Paducah.

County Court House, Paducah, Ky.

GRANT'S OCCUPATION OF PADUCAH

PROCLAMATION,
TO THE CITIZENS OF

PADUCAH!

I have come among you, not as an enemy, but as your friend and fellow-citizen, not to injure or annoy you, but to respect the rights, and to defend and enforce the rights of all loyal citizens. An enemy, in rebellion against our common Government, has taken possession of, and planted its guns upon the soil of Kentucky and fired upon our flag. Hickman and Columbus are in his hands. He is moving upon your city. I am here to defend you against this enemy and to assert and maintain the authority and sovereignty of your Government and mine. I have nothing to do with opinions. I shall deal only with armed rebellion and its aiders and abetors. You can pursue your usual avocations without fear or hindrance. The strong arm of the Government is here to protect its friends, and to punish only its enemies. Whenever it is manifest that you are able to defend yourselves, to maintain the authority of your Government and protect the rights of all its loyal citizens, I shall withdraw the forces under my command from your city.

U. S. GRANT,
Brig. Gen. U. S. A., Commanding.

Paducah, Sept 6th. 1861.

Early in the Civil War, U.S. Army Brigadier-General Ulysses S. Grant identified Paducah as a critical point for the Federal army to occupy and control as part of its campaign to dominate the Mississippi River Valley.

On September 6, 1861, Grant and his army moved toward Paducah, Grant traveling by gunboat and his troops marching to the Illinois shore across from the northern section of Paducah. At this spot 114 coal barges were joined together with boards to form a pontoon bridge, over which the army and all its supplies crossed. As soon as the soldiers reached the Kentucky shore, meal tents were set up. Later in the afternoon, 5,000 soldiers lined up behind mounted officers and four bands and marched to Seventh and Broadway. Turning down Broadway, the army marched four abreast while the bands played the tune "Union Forever."

As soon as General Grant arrived in Paducah, he issued a proclamation to reassure the local citizens. In this proclamation, he promised the people of Paducah that he was not there to "injure or annoy" but to preserve their rights as "loyal citizens." Knowing that most of Paducah's "loyal citizens" were actually sympathetic to the Southern cause, Grant's probable reason for issuing the proclamation was to notify the people of Paducah that the Federal army was in control of the town for the duration of the war.

Grant put Brigadier-General E. A. Payne in charge of the town and returned immediately to Cairo, Illinois. In his dispatch to Major General John Fremont describing his occupation of Paducah, Grant noted that he had taken possession of the telegraph office, railroad depot, and marine hospital and had discovered a large quantity of rations and leather goods meant for the Southern army.

Firmly under Northern control, Paducah served as an important supply distribution point for the Union army during campaigns in Tennessee, Mississippi, and Georgia. Paducah avoided gunfire until 1864, when Northern and Southern soldiers met at the Battle of Paducah.

BATTLE OF PADUCAH

After the Union army occupied Paducah in 1861, the soldiers built a military fortification around the existing marine hospital and named it Fort Anderson, in honor of the Union commander at Fort Sumter. The fort's location was on the northern boundary of the town and overlooked the Ohio River. The fort served as the headquarters for the soldiers stationed in Paducah, who were probably not expecting to see much action in the war.

In March of 1864, Southern General Nathan B. Forrest and 1,800 calvarymen moved toward Paducah. The soldiers crossed into Paducah on March 25th and regrouped at a spot where the Katterjohn Building now stands. Their purpose was to capture Fort Anderson and occupy Paducah, thereby cutting supply lines to Union armies fighting in Georgia.

In an effort to avoid bloodshed, six southern soldiers who were from Paducah carried a message from Forrest to the commander at Fort Anderson, Colonel Stephen Hicks. Forrest's message requested Hick's surrender and promised "if I have to storm your works, you may expect no quarter." Hicks responded that he had to "respectfully decline surrendering as you may require" and the battle was on.

Around 4:30 pm, Forrest issued the command "forward men, and mix with 'em." Approaching the fort, the southern soldiers discovered 50-foot ditches surrounding it on all exposed sides. Unable to cross the ditches, the soldiers withdrew, then stormed the fort a second time. Each time, the soldiers met heavy gunfire from the 600 Union soldiers inside the fort and barrage from gunboats on the Ohio River. Unable to penetrate the fort, the soldiers entered residences surrounding the fort and began firing into the fort from second-floor windows. Realizing that it was impossible to capture the fort, Forrest ordered a retreat.

A total of 25 men were killed and 85 wounded during the battle. A major blow to the southern forces was the death of Colonel A. P. Thompson, who was struck by a cannonball while mounted on his horse. Thompson was a resident of Paducah who had served as Commonwealth Attorney before the war started. He had been given the honor of leading the charge on his hometown.

Paducah's greatest loss was the destruction of 60 homes in the Lower Town neighborhood. Colonel Hicks ordered the burning of "all homes in musket range of the fort from which the sharpshooters of the enemy fired upon us yesterday." This action proved needless since Forrest and his troops had retreated and did not renew their attack on Fort Anderson.

Harper's Weekly *drawing of Fort Anderson.*

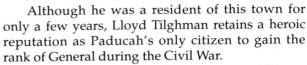

GENERAL LLOYD TILGHMAN

Although he was a resident of this town for only a few years, Lloyd Tilghman retains a heroic reputation as Paducah's only citizen to gain the rank of General during the Civil War.

Lloyd Tilghman was born to one of Maryland's leading families in 1816. He was a graduate of West Point and fought as a captain in the Mexican War. As a civilian, he worked first as a civil engineer for the Baltimore and Susquehanna Railroad. He and his family moved to Paducah in 1852 and he became the chief surveyor for the New Orleans and Ohio Railroad. He was an active member of the Grace Episcopal Church and made stained-glass windows for the church building.

When the Civil War broke out, Tilghman first served as a colonel in the Kentucky State Guard, a militia group that was charged with preserving Kentucky's neutrality. He later joined the Confederate side and organized the Third Kentucky Regiment. Promoted to the rank of Brigadier-General, Tilghman was given command of Fort Henry on the Tennessee River and Fort Donelson on the Cumberland. Facing overwhelming forces, Tilghman surrendered Fort Donelson in 1863 and served as a prisoner of war for six months.

Upon his release, Tilghman was given command of 10,000 soldiers in Mississippi and charged with helping to protect Vicksburg, a critical southern town on the Mississippi River. While engaged in battle with Federal forces near Champion's Hill on May 16, 1863, Tilghman was struck by a cannonball and died later that day from his wound.

In 1909, Lloyd Tilghman's family erected a bronze statue of him in Lang Park that serves as a reminder of his remarkable life.

Confederate Memorial, General Lloyd Tilghman's Monument, Paducah, Ky.

1871–1890

Paducah had survived the Civil War. The town moved into the Victorian era with an emphasis on industrial development as the means to build and sustain the local economy.

Paducah was fortunate to be set up to manufacture and distribute a broad range of goods and products. These included lumber products, iron implements, farm tools, buggies, food products, including vinegar, rope and cord, harness and leather goods, and pottery. A healthy economic atmosphere also led to the establishment of five new financial institutions, all of which built impressive banking houses in downtown Paducah.

Agriculture also continued to be important to the local economy. Paducah soon became the largest dark-tobacco market and inspection center in Kentucky and by 1889 eight tobacco-processing facilities were located here.

The optimism in the post-war period was reflected in several important construction projects. The local Episcopal denomination built the magnificent new Grace Episcopal Church. Two major public buildings went up in 1882 — the Paducah City Hall and the U. S. Post Office and Customs House. These three substantial buildings displayed an image of a community that was progressive and prosperous.

Paducah was a growing community and in 1884 the town limits were extended to Twenty-fifth Street. Families were building substantial residences in the Lower Town and Upper Town neighborhoods and along Broadway and Jefferson Street. These beautiful homes were designed in the Italianate, Queen Anne, Romanesque, and Eastlake styles.

RIVERS AND RAILROADS

The rivers and the railroads supported Paducah's economic growth in the second half of the nineteenth century. The importance of the local waterways industry is demonstrated by the fact that between 1870 and 1900 one-third of Paducah's population had jobs connected to the river and its industries. With such facilities as the Paducah Marine Ways and the Paducah Boat-Building Company, the town maintained the largest boat-building operation on the Ohio River. Packet lines owned by Paducahans, such as the Fowler Brothers organization, provided fast and cheap transportation for passengers and cargo. This was truly the golden period of the rivers for Paducah.

The railroads were also becoming increasingly important to the local economy. In the 1870s, the New Orleans and Ohio Railroad provided a regular rail connection to Union City, Tennessee, and the railway lines to the south. The need for access to eastern railway lines led the local town council to subscribe $100,000 toward the construction of a railroad line between Paducah and Elizabethtown. This railway later became part of the Illinois Central system, which maintained a hospital for employees and shops for locomotive maintenance in Paducah. By 1900, the Illinois Central facility was the largest industry in Paducah.

Scene at Wharf Boat, Paducah, Ky.

FOWLER BROTHERS & COMPANY

A symbolic high point of Paducah's riverboat history came in March 1881 when Fowler Brothers & Company joined with John Gilbert and the Evansville, Cairo and Memphis Steam Company to create the Paducah & Cairo Packet Company. This company was chartered with a $25,000 capital stock to operate a packet service on the Ohio and Mississippi rivers.

During the heyday of the river packets from 1870 to 1910, the Fowler Brothers' boats were among the fastest and best-known on the river. The steamer Joe Fowler operated from 1881 to 1912 and ran between Paducah and Evansville, Indiana. The steamer Dick Fowler was built in Jeffersonville, Indiana in 1893 and ran between Paducah and Cairo, Illinois from 1893 to 1912. Famous as one of the fastest boats on the river, the Dick Fowler raced the steamer Spread Eagle from Cairo to Paducah, reaching Paducah in 2 hours and 17 minutes and beating the Spread Eagle by 9 minutes.

The steamer packets remained active until the early 1900s when the railroads gradually displaced the rivers as the chief mode of transportation for passengers and cargo.

> **Regular Mail Boat!**
>
> Steamer J. S. HOPKINS
>
> Str. JOE FOWLER.
>
> Daily Except Sunday at 9:30 o'clock, Morning.
>
> **FOR   EVANSVILLE !**
>
> Arriving at Evansville at 10:30 o'clock, Next Morning.
>
> Carrying U. S. Mail and Adams Express.
>
> SAFETY! SPEED! COMFORT!

The Joe Fowler.

GRACE EPISCOPAL CHURCH

Grace Episcopal Church, Paducah, Kentucky

One of the first major construction projects in Paducah after the Civil War was the erection of the Grace Episcopal Church on Broadway.

The Episcopal church denomination had been organized in Paducah in 1846. In 1848, a frame structure was brought down the river from Louisville and erected on the west side of Market Street for use as the first Grace Episcopal Church. This building was damaged during the Civil War when it was used as a hospital for Union soldiers.

Following the war, the Episcopalians made a commitment to build a new church building and purchased a lot on Broadway. The church commissioned New York architect Henry Congdon to design the new church building in the popular High Gothic style. The cornerstone of the church building was laid in 1873.

Church traditions maintain that Congdon prepared two sets of blueprints of varying scale and grandeur for the new structure. Inadvertently, the wrong set of blueprints was used, resulting in a building much larger than originally planned by the vestry of the church. The church was able to finish the construction of the church building in 1874 but it took many years to furnish the church and to install the beautiful stained-glass windows. For many years, the members continued to use the original church's old pews, which had been nicked and dented from the horses and mules of Union soldiers.

The Grace Episcopal Church is now the oldest church structure in Paducah. The many beautiful details of the building include the bell tower topped by a cross, the purple and green slate roof, and the dark interior woodwork.

The Grace Episcopal Church has been listed on the National Register of Historic Places.

CAST-IRON STOREFRONTS

Economic prosperity in Paducah and the town's growth as a retail and service center led to the construction of many new commercial buildings in the downtown area between 1870 and 1900. These two- and three-story brick buildings were designed in the popular Italianate style, complete with cast-iron storefronts and highly ornamental window hoods and cornices.

The facade of a typical downtown commercial building had two distinct parts. The first floor was composed of a cast-iron storefront that had been manufactured at a local iron foundry. The storefront was always flush to the sidewalk and had a slightly recessed central doorway. Some buildings had a side entrance that led to the upper floors, which were used as living quarters for the owner and his family. The upper floor facade had tall, narrow windows

The DuBois-Robertson Drug Store at 412 Broadway.

topped with decorative sheet-metal hoods, usually in the form of segmented or round arches. The facade was topped by a sheet-metal cornice that often bore the name of the building's owner or the nature of the business.

The distinctive cast-iron storefronts and sheet-metal details were manufactured at local iron foundries, such as the J. H. Johnson & Co. Foundry (founded in 1855) and the Linning & Jackson foundry (founded in 1869).

By 1900, almost every downtown Paducah commercial building had a cast-iron storefront. Many of these storefronts displayed an interesting detail, a raised arrow motif, that perhaps was an allusion to Paducah's Indian heritage.

The cast-iron storefronts were manufactured and shipped in pieces and then assembled at the site. This made it easy to distribute cast-iron storefronts manufactured in Paducah to many nearby towns, such as Metropolis, Princeton, Arlington, and Cadiz.

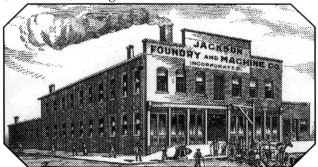

Linning and Jackson Foundry at First Street and Kentucky Avenue.

OAK GROVE CEMETERY

In the nineteenth century, the romantic spirit of the age found its most poignant expression in graveyard architecture and its associated monuments.

Established in 1847, Oak Grove Cemetery is Paducah's great Victorian burial place. Laid out like a city, the grassy lanes have been given appropriate names like Peace, Silent, and Grace. Many of the most famous individuals in Paducah's history are buried here. The striking entrance, with its iron gateway and small octagonal caretaker's cottage, was added during the administration of Mayor James P. Smith in the first decade of this century.

Reflecting its 145 years of existence, Oak Grove Cemetery has funerary sculpture dating from every period of the community's past. One early monument is the 1841 James January headstone, decorated with carvings of weeping willow trees, a tabletomb and an obelisk. Other markers display explicit Victorian symbols for death and mourning, like severed tree trunks, scattered books, lilies, garlands, and harps. Several markers are topped by stone anchors, representing a life anchored in Christ. There are also some remarkable pieces of statuary, including beautifully carved angels, draped urns, and towering obelisks.

Several prominent Paducah families commissioned private mausoleums as their final resting places. Most are done in the Romanesque style with massive stonework and intricate detailing. One striking exception is the Smith family mausoleum, which is purely classical in design.

The magnificent markers and mausoleums at Oak Grove Cemetery were executed locally by such firms as the Hilke and Hartz Monuments Works, the J. E. Williamson Marble Works and the Beasley Monument Company. The stone carvers at these companies were truly artists and their stone legacies are an important part of Paducah's cultural past.

Entrance to Oak Grove Cemetery, Paducah, Ky.

POST OFFICE AND THE CITY HALL — 1882

Two of Paducah's most impressive buildings were constructed in 1882, the U. S. Custom House and Post Office and the Paducah City Hall (illustrated on page 8).

Located at the northwest corner of Fifth Street and Broadway, the Custom House was the finest Romanesque Revival structure ever constructed in Paducah. Besides housing the local postal operations, the three-story building contained governmental offices and the United States courtrooms. A major addition was made to the west side of the building. The statue of Chief Paduke was originally located in front of the building.

The structure was demolished in 1937 and replaced by a Classical Revival-style post office and governmental building. The stonework from the 1882 building was salvaged and reused to build a residence in the western section of Paducah and a church on Farley Place. The stone eagle that rested on a parapet of the building was rescued and reused on the 1937 Flood memorial on Jefferson Street.

The Paducah city government hired local architect D. A. McKinnon to design a new city hall in 1882. Built at the corner of Fourth Street and Kentucky Avenue, the new city hall cost $20,000. The building had a rectangular plan with monumental steps leading up to the entrances on the north and south sides. A central tower contained a bell and displayed a four-sided clock. In a monumental feat of engineering, the roof and tower of the building were lifted and a third story was added in 1909.

The 1882 Paducah City Hall was demolished shortly after the construction of the 1965 city hall building.

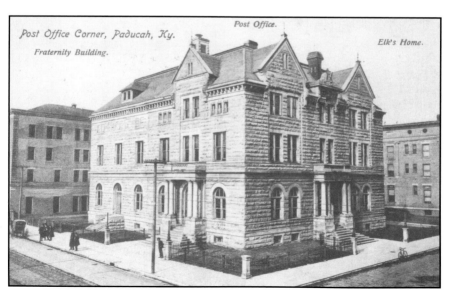

Post Office Corner, Paducah, Ky.

Fraternity Building.

Post Office.

Elk's Home.

ELECTRIC STREETCARS COME TO TOWN

The landscape of Paducah changed in 1890 when the first electric streetcar was introduced to the community. This was only the second electric streetcar system in the state, a fact that reflects Paducah's progressive nature at that time.

Local citizens had ridden on mule-drawn streetcars since 1872. This first streetcar line ran along South Locust Street (now Third Street) from Broadway to Broad Street. Other early routes ran down Broadway to the Railroad Depot at Eleventh Street and down Sixth Street and then down Trimble Street (now Park Avenue) to Oak Grove Cemetery.

A new period in local transportation history began when the first electric streetcar ran in Paducah on July 4, 1890. In 1892, the city government passed several ordinances governing the streetcar lines. No fare for riding the streetcar could exceed five cents and cars had to run at least every hour and between the hours of 6:00 am and 10:00 pm. The cars could not exceed speeds of 8 miles per hour within the downtown business district and 10 miles per hour elsewhere.

By the 1920s, 13 electric streetcars ran on 18 miles of track that extended to the Paducah Country Club, Oak Grove Cemetery, Rowlandtown, Union Station, the end of Guthrie Avenue and across Island Creek. This period of Paducah history neared its end in the late 1920s as the streetcar lines were converted to bus routes.

Fourth and Broadway looking east, circa 1920.

1891–1910

At the turn of the century, Paducah continued to enjoy the fruits of its self-generated economic growth. The city government had an unrestrictive attitude toward business and the community welcomed many new entrepreneurs who started new enterprises. By 1900, Paducah had become the second largest manufacturing and distributing center in Kentucky. Two years later, the town had grown sufficiently in size and population to be designated as a second-class city with a new city charter. Paducah had passed that undefinable point of changing from a town to a city.

Accompanying this period of economic prosperity was a trend toward more spectacular public buildings. In Paducah, monumental public buildings constructed between 1891 and 1910 included the Palmer House Hotel, Carnegie Public Library, Market House, Union Depot, Paducah High School (see page 4), Broadway Methodist Church, Temple Israel, First Christian Church, Central Fire Station, Riverside Hospital, and the Elks Lodge. This was the golden age of architecture in Paducah and some of the community's finest buildings came from this period.

Three important advances were made during these decades. By the 1890s, the public school system had grown to include nine schools, including two that were designated for black students. The city government provided civic improvements like paved streets, sidewalks, a water system, and fire protection. The period ended with the construction of two magnificent bank buildings in downtown Paducah. One was the Beaux-Arts style First National Bank Building at Third and Broadway (see page 4) and the other was the City National Bank Building at Fourth and Broadway, commonly known as the Ten Story Building.

"Bide-a-wee" Summer Home, Mayor J. P. Smith, Paducah, Ky.

PALMER HOUSE HOTEL

One of Paucah's great hotels, the Palmer House, was built between 1891 and 1892 at the corner of Fifth and Broadway. The finished hotel cost $135,000 for the construction and $35,000 for the furnishings.

The man credited with spearheading the development of the Palmer House was Charles Reed, the former proprietor of the Richmond House Hotel at First and Broadway. Desiring a new hotel to operate, Reed secured the financial backing of a New York investor.

After the foundation and basement had been laid and the first floor built, the New York investor went bankrupt and construction stopped. The half-finished hotel stood empty until Reed was able to purchase it at a bankruptcy sale. Local investors were organized to finish the project, including Elbridge Palmer who pledged $7,000 providing the hotel would bear his name. This is how the Palmer House was named.

Four stories in height and constructed of solid brick masonry, the Palmer House can be classified as Paducah's first "skyscraper." Two technological advancements of the 1880's, passenger elevators and central steam heat, were incorporated into the design of the hotel. Bay windows on the upper floors of the North Fifty street facade provided light and additional space to the front rooms. When the hotel opened, rooms rented for $2, $2.50, and $3.

In all, the hotel contained 25 guest rooms, 18 suite rooms, 6 staircases, and 9 bathing rooms, plus each floor had a bathroom. The hotel was lit with 600 gas jets and heated by steam that was guaranteed to heat the hotel to 70 degrees in zero weather.

The newspaper article about the opening of the new hotel in 1892 concluded: "The hotel in short, in all ways, architectural in particular, and convenience and elegance in general, is all that judgment and taste and money could possibly have made it."

The Palmer House was demolished in the late 1950s and replaced with modern commercial structures.

Palmer Hotel, Paducah, Ky.

LIFE IN PADUCAH IN 1904

What kind of town was Paducah at the turn of the century? What were the issues and concerns of Paducah's citizens 90 years ago? One document that illustrates life at this time is the 1904 Ordinance and Municipal Laws book for the City of Paducah. This is a record of all the laws and regulations passed by the city council of Paducah. Among the interesting and fun regulations on the books in 1904 are:

IT WAS UNLAWFUL TO clean out the contents of a privy between May and October without the written permission of the mayor.

IT WAS UNLAWFUL TO sell or throw confetti, talcum powder, flour or similar products.

IT WAS UNLAWFUL TO sell or give away any "spirituous, vinous or malt liquor" to any woman, minor or habitual drunkard.

IT WAS UNLAWFUL FOR anyone working for the telegraph or telephone companies to deliver a message concerning the results of a horse race.

IT WAS UNLAWFUL FOR any person or persons to loiter or loaf on the streets of Paducah or in public places. An exemption was made for businessmen who were allowed to stand or sit in front of their own property.

IT WAS UNLAWFUL TO remove a corpse from the the city by railroad, steamboat or private conveyance unless it was accompanied by a death certificate signed by the attending physician or the city physician.

IT WAS UNLAWFUL FOR any female to enter or frequent any saloon within the city limits or to loiter in such a saloon.

IT WAS UNLAWFUL TO fly kites in the streets of Paducah or to play ball games within 200 feet of any house.

IT WAS UNLAWFUL TO ride a horse on any street in Paducah at a gait faster than a trot.

IT WAS UNLAWFUL FOR one person to transport another person to a polling place on election day. People riding on streetcars to polling places also had to pay their own fare.

WALLACE PARK

Wallace Park was a popular amusement park and recreational area developed in the western section of the town in the early part of this century. The park was created by the local trolley company as an impetus for riders on land that had been the Phillip Wallace farm.

Wallace Park was developed by the Paducah Traction Company, which in 1911 maintained 17 miles of streetcar track and more than 30 streetcars. The company promised "polite service, comfortable cars and prompt schedules." In its advertisements, the company urged the public to "take the trolley to beautiful WALLACE PARK, an ideal pleasure resort where rest or recreation may be enjoyed and life-giving air inhaled." The company boasted that Wallace Park could be reached by trolley from "any part of the city or suburbs" for a five cent fare.

On a typical weekend, a single motorcar would haul up to 15 open trailer cards loaded with people to the park. Attractions at the park included a zoo, lake, casino, baseball fields, pavilion, and theater. The zoo contained bears, monkeys and eagles. The theater and pavilion could seat 600 people and the casino was occasionally used by stock companies for performances. The first country club in Paducah was established at the southeast corner of the park and included a clubhouse and a nine-hole golf course.

The use of Wallace Park declined in the 1920s and in 1925 the land was platted and sold for residential development. Around this time, the City of Paducah purchased land and developed Bob Noble Park as a public park facility.

The Lakes, Wallace Park, Paducah, Ky.

WHITE WEEK

Paducah suffered one of the most beautiful but miserable periods in its history in 1902 when "White Week" took place.

After a month of unusually pleasant weather, heavy rain turned to snow and sleet on Sunday, January 26th. The precipitation soon covered all exterior objects with two inches of snow and ice. A heavy rain fell on the following Tuesday, causing the weight of the heavily-packed snow to shift and tear the roofs off of buildings. On Wednesday morning, building owners and merchants all over Paducah found holes in roofs and building contents being ruined by water. Later that day, the rain turned to ice and trees and telephone poles began falling from the weight.

Soon, the city lost all of its telephone and telegraph service and fire alarm boxes were put out of service. Each street corner was a tangle of wires and cables and broken poles. All electrical power was turned off in the city due to the fallen wires, meaning streetcars stopped on their tracks. No local newspaper was printed for the first time since the Civil War. All business and activities were suspended and the streets were deserted.

Snow began falling again on Wednesday night and the town woke up on Thursday morning to a magnificent but wrecked city as everything outside was covered with ice and snow. A contemporary description records that *"Every twig was a fairy wand, with a diamond tip. Every wire was a glittering necklace of jewels, festooning the street. Ice covered all things beautifying the commonplace and almost causing one to forget the ruin that had been wrought."*

The city slowly came back to life as a thaw set in and by February 4th electrical power and the streetcar service had been restored. More than 250 workers labored to restore the electrical poles and to rehang wires and cables. The local telephone system was almost completely destroyed and the final damage estimate for the city was around $200,000.

A recorder of the wonders of "White Week" admitted that the week was a combination of "delights and horrors" but argued that nobody but a "stark lunatic or an arctic explorer" would want to repeat it.

Broken wires on Fifth Street, looking north from Washington. White Week. ©*John T. Lane.*

CARNEGIE PUBLIC LIBRARY

The great promoter of the public library movement at the turn of the century was industrialist Andrew Carnegie, whose foundation provided seed money for the creation of hundreds of libraries in America.

A $35,000 donation from the Carnegie Foundation funded a public library for Paducah. The City of Paducah purchased a lot at Ninth and Broadway for the construction of this library and the library opened to the public on October 4, 1904.

The Classical Revival structure housing the Carnegie Library was designed by local architect A. L. Lassiter and ranks as one of his great architectural achievements. A monumental flight of steps led up to the front entrance. Four Ionic columns supported the front portico that displayed the words CARNEGIE PUBLIC LIBRARY. After passing through the arched entranceway, the visitor entered into an atrium area that was lit from above by a rotunda. Reading rooms located on both sides of the atrium had huge arched windows providing light. The interior space also had marble pilasters, stenciled walls with drawings of great literary figures, and arched openings between sections of the library.

The Carnegie Library served generations of book lovers until it was closed after a fire in the mid-1960s. Following a lengthy public debate, the decision was made to build a new library structure instead of restoring the old one. The Carnegie Library was demolished. Fortunately, the library lot was purchased by the Grace Episcopal Church which maintains it as a green place in the downtown area.

The Carnegie Library now survives only in the memories of citizens who remember it as one of the most elegant buildings ever constructed in Paducah.

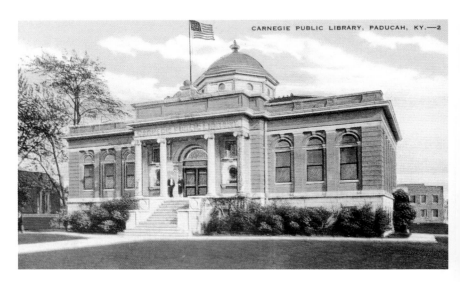

CARNEGIE PUBLIC LIBRARY, PADUCAH, KY.—2

MARKET HOUSE

Unlike most downtown areas that developed around a courthouse square, Paducah's downtown grew up around the Market House. The first market house was a frame structure built in 1836. This was replaced in 1850 with a brick building. The current Market House was built in 1905 and was designed by local architect W. L. Brainerd and constructed by local contractor George Katterjohn. The $25,000 building was designed in the Classical Revival style and exhibited such details as pilasters, garlands, pediments, and egg-and-dart molding.

The Market House was always owned and operated by the town government and a special set of ordinances controlled activities here. Among the laws established by the town government:

THE MARKET HOUSE was defined as a market place for the sale and purchase of provisions, vegetables and other articles necessary for the subsistence, comfort and convenience of the inhabitants of the town.

THE MARKET WAS TO BE open every day except Sunday. A bell was run for the opening of the market at 5:00am (4:00 in the summer months) and the market remained open for 3 hours. The market also opened on Saturday afternoons from 2:00 to 9:00 pm.

A MARKET MASTER was responsible for superintending the market and for "keeping it thoroughly cleaned and in good order." He was compensated $600 per year for his labors.

DOGS WERE NOT ALLOWED in the market house unless they were confined and kept out of the way by their owner.

In the 1960s, the city declared the Market House operations to be unsanitary and closed it. From efforts by a group of concerned citizens, it has since developed as a cultural center for the community.

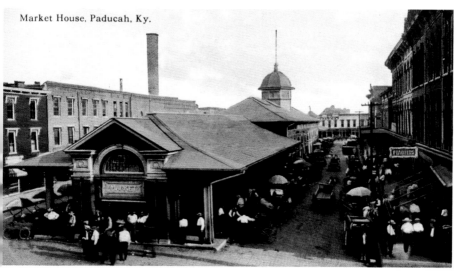

Market House, Paducah, Ky.

MONUMENTS IN PADUCAH

Early in the twentieth century, America was in the mood to remember and commemorate its past. This mood led to the commissioning of monuments dedicated to heroic figures that were to be displayed in public places — in front of county courthouses and post offices, at entrances to parks, in public squares, and along newly-planned boulevards and avenues.

One popular area of commemoration was to look back and honor a town's beginnings. In 1909, the local chapter of the Daughters of the American Revolution erected a statue of Chief Paduke by Chicago sculptor Lorado Taft. The commemorative statue had a functional aspect with the inclusion of drinking fountain basins that protruded from the base of the statue. The Chief Paduke statue originally stood in front of the Post Office at 5th and Broadway but was moved to the Jefferson Street boulevard after the 1937 Flood.

Many pieces of statuary that were erected at this time focused on figures and actions connected to the Civil War, which had created a new mythology of heroism for Americans. Groups and families worked to remember the "gallant sacrifices" made by the heroes of the war. In Paducah, the family of General Lloyd Tilghman commissioned a bronze statue of him by noted sculptor Henry Kittson. Erected in 1912 in the middle of Lang Park, the statue stands on a granite base donated by the United Daughters of the Confederacy organization.

Other distinctive monuments in Paducah were the Animal Drinking Fountain at Tenth and Broadway, the Oscar Turner Fountain in front of the Carnegie Library, the World War I veterans monument in Oak Grove Cemetery, and the Flood Memorial on the Jefferson Street boulevard.

Drinking Fountain, Tenth and Broadway, erected by The D. A. R., Paducah, Ky.

1911–1930

Paducah started and ended this period with big celebrations, one to mark a special homecoming event and the other to celebrate the long-awaited construction of an automobile bridge across the Ohio River.

While enjoying these celebrations and noting the construction of several remarkable buildings, Paducah began to experience a slowdown in its economic growth. Several important local industries suffered financial reverses or were permanently closed. These include such economic mainstays as tobacco-processing plants, distilleries, lumber companies and riverboat lines.

By the 1920s, the railroads were overshadowing the river industry as the mainstay of the Paducah economy. This position was solidified by the construction of new Illinois Central shops in Paducah, an $11 million project that resulted in the largest railroad plant in the nation. Another advancement was the construction of a $4 million railroad bridge across the Ohio River in 1918 that directly connected Paducah to the Illinois Central rail lines to the north.

Several remarkable buildings were constructed in Paducah between 1911 and 1930. In 1927, construction began on the nine-story Hotel Irvin Cobb, which opened in 1929 and soon dominated both the downtown Paducah skyline and the community's social life. Also built in 1927 was the Columbia Theater, an exuberant movie palace that reflected the American public's love for motion pictures.

These two decades ended appropriately with the local celebration of the construction of the Paducah-Brookport Bridge which finally provided automobile access between Kentucky and Illinois. The parade that marked the opening of this bridge on May 8, 1929, was the city's last celebration before the dark days of the Depression hit.

HOME-COMING WEEK

A special "Home-coming Week" was planned for May 19-24, 1913, when 5,000 visitors returned home for reunions and celebrations and the opportunity to enjoy Paducah's hospitality. The idea of a "Home-coming Week" came from Colonel Ben Weille and the community spent months planning special events.

Each night of the special week featured a parade. One night had elaborate floats sponsored by local businesses and manufacturers and another night had a burlesque night. Jefferson Street was transformed into a carnival with rides and booths. The merry-go-round ran for 16 hours each day.

We're Expecting You

Back in Old Paducah for the

Home Coming May 19-24

And expect you to assist in welcoming Chief Paduke on his first visit in a century. If you haven't been home in years you'll be surprised.

There Will be Something Doing All the Time

Hydroaeroplane flights, fireworks, flower parades, band Concerts are just a few of the amusements features.

All Free! Don't Hesitate to Bring Your Friends

The crowning event of the week was the triumphant return of Chief Paduke to the town. Summoned by shrieking factory whistles and a booming cannon, Chief Paduke and his party crossed the Ohio River from Illinois on the steamer G. W. Robertson.

Chief Paduke actually was local attorney James G. Wheeler, covered in paint and feathers and impersonating the legendary Indian. After disembarking at the riverfront, Chief Paduke mounted a white horse and rode down Broadway to a platform erected at the corner of Fifth and Broadway. A crowd of 15,000 people watched Mayor Thomas Hazelip greet the chief with the words, "Take Paducah, it is yours."

James G. Wheeler portraying Chief Paduke.

ILLINOIS CENTRAL RAILROAD SHOPS

Ground was broken on March 15, 1924 for the expansion of the Illinois Central railroad shops in Paducah. The $11 million project resulted in the construction of 23 buildings and creation of a complex covering 110 acres. When completed in 1927, the site was one of the four largest industrial plants in Kentucky and the largest construction and repair plant constructed by a railroad.

Part of the site for the shops was created by filling in a large ravine that extended from Washington Street to Jones Street. In 190 days, 625,000 cubic feet of dirt was moved by train cars from a site in McCracken County. A total of 44,560 carloads of dirt was hauled in to fill the hollow.

The principal operation of the new Illinois Central shops was the remanufacture and maintenance of locomotives. The railroad shops became Paducah's largest employer and in 1938 had 1,075 people on the payroll.

In the 1940s, the equipment at the shops was converted from serving steam engines to diesel engines. Throughout the 1940s and 1950s, the I. C. slowly switched over from steam to diesel-powered locomotives. In 1967, the I. C. railroad chose Paducah as the site to repair its aging diesel fleet. In the 1980s, the I. C. shops became the home of the P. & L. Railroad and VMV Enterprises, operations which continue Paducah's railroad heritage.

Illinois Central Railroad Shops, Paducah, Kentucky
Ohio and Tennessee Rivers in Background

BOB NOBLE PARK

Local demands for recreational space led the City of Paducah to develop Bob Noble Park in the 1920s. 105 acres of land for a park were purchased by park commissioners in 1915 for $25,000. The land remained unimproved until the mid-1920s when Captain Bob Noble donated $10,000 toward development of a municipal park. The city matched this amount and the new park opened in 1926.

Improvements to the park included a concrete wall running along the front of the park, an ornamental stone entranceway, a wire fence enclosing the grounds and a driveway circling the park. A stream was dammed up to create a lake that was stocked with fish. A bandstand was built at the edge of the lake.

At the entranceway, tablets were placed recognizing the park commissioner and the project architect, D. Harry Jamieson. Another tablet recognized Bob Noble with the words:

"Native of Paducah, life-long resident, patriotic Kentuckian, Southern gentleman, whose generosity made possible the beautifying of the playgrounds for the people of his hometown, this tablet is gratefully and affectionately dedicated, 1926."

In the 1930s, a swimming pool and pool house were added to the park as a WPA relief project. By the 1950s, an amusement park known as Funland had been added to the park. Generations of children loved the ferris wheel, miniature train, carousel and pony rides. One special feature of the park was the old-fashioned fire engine that would pick up children and deliver them to Funland for birthday parties and special celebrations.

Today, efforts are being made by the City of Paducah to revitalize and beautify Noble Park for future generations.

Lake in Bob Noble Park
Paducah, Ky.

COLUMBIA THEATER

The Columbia Theater stands as a testament to America's love for the movies in the 1920s and 1930s.

This movie palace was built by the Keiler family who owned several local theaters, including the Arcade theater at the corner of Fifth and Broadway. Built in 1911, the Arcade was the first theater in Paducah built specifically for motion pictures. It was located in the one-story Arcade building, which also housed shops that faced the open interior courtyard that led up to the theater's entrance.

In 1927, Leo Keiler built the larger and grander Columbia Theater. This brick building has an elaborate facade composed of blue and white terra cotta tiles. This facade displays an eclectic assortment of architectural details, including spiraled Byzantine columns, classical urns, friezes and capitals, and busts of Greek goddesses. The original Columbia sign was 50 feet tall and was lit with 5,000 light bulbs.

The Columbia Theater opened on April 18, 1927, when 2,000 fortunate patrons had tickets to see Clara Bow starring in IT and hear Jack Adams on the Barton console organ. The theater was one of the first in America to feature "Vitaphone" sound. The Columbia and Arcade theaters were especially popular in the summer months where "air cooled" systems kept patrons free from perspiration.

Paducah's downtown movie theaters closed in the 1980s and these buildings now await redevelopment for exciting new uses.

Irvin S. Cobb certainly merits the title of Paducah's favorite native son. And in return, Paducah has received world-wide fame as the beloved home of Irvin S. Cobb.

Many titles can be assigned to Cobb — writer, humorist, raconteur, local colorist, reporter, autobiographer, actor, master of ceremonies — but probably his favorite title was simply "Duke of Paducah."

Born in 1876 in his grandfather's home on South Third Street, Cobb displayed his intelligence and talents at an early age. When he was 16 he began writing for the *Paducah Daily News*. His first story was on the availability and costs of rabbits at the Market House. By the age of 18 he was the head reporter at the newspaper. In his reporting work, he got to know many of the colorful local characters who would later inspire his short stories and humorous anecdotes.

After working at newspapers in Louisville and Paducah, Cobb went to New York City and started writing for the *Evening Sun*. He was soon promoted to feature writing and the Sunday papers included many of his humorous articles. In 1911, he joined the staff at the *Saturday Evening Post* and began publishing his short stories. His most famous stories dealt with Judge Priest, a figure based on Paducah's Judge William Bishop. Ten short stories about Judge Priest were printed in a book under the title *Back Home*.

IRVIN COBB'S MONUMENT IN OAK GROVE CEMETERY, PADUCAH, KY.—36

IRVIN SHREWSBURY COBB
1876 — 1944
"BACK HOME"

Irvin Cobb published his first novel in 1922 and this was followed by novels and short story collections throughout the 1920s and 1930s. In his spare time, Cobb also appeared in the movies, including one appearance with Will Rogers in *Steamboat Round the Bend*. He also served as the master of ceremonies at the 1935 Academy Awards and presented Shirley Temple with her special Oscar.

Cobb died in 1944 in New York and was brought back to Paducah for burial. At his request, his ashes were buried at Oak Grove Cemetery and the spot was marked by a large granite boulder with the simple epitaph "Back Home."

HOTEL IRVIN COBB

By the 1920s, Americans were traveling across the country in automobiles on the newly-developed systems of highways and parkways. Accommodating this traveling public were large hotels located in the downtown areas of towns and cities.

Paducah's great hotel of this period was the Irvin Cobb. The Cobb was built by local entrepreneur Adolph Weil at a cost of $400,000 and designed by Chicago architect Walter Alschlager. Weil named the hotel for his good friend and writer Irvin Cobb, who remarked on the opening day: "From lobby to roof garden, there is no hotel on this continent nor in this world more exquisitely designed."

The Cobb Hotel soon became the social center for Paducah as functions were held in the hotel's ballroom and dining room. Dances were often held on the roof garden and crowds would gather on the streets below to listen to the live music. The Cobb even served as a refugee and governmental center during the 1937 Flood.

HOTEL IRVIN COBB, PADUCAH, KY.—14

The Cobb Hotel was designed in the Tudor Revival style. It was built with a steel frame faced with Kentucky limestone on the first two floors and brown brick on the upper floors. Projecting from the building's east and north facades were panels of brick covered with stucco and wood timbering.

After a period of being vacant in the 1970s, the hotel was restored for senior citizen housing in 1979. The ballroom and dining room once again serve as important social centers for the community.

PADUCAH-BROOKPORT BRIDGE

For many years, the citizens of Paducah dreamed of a vehicle bridge across the Ohio River to Illinois. Access to Illinois was only available by ferry service or by the railroad bridge constructed in 1918.

In the late 1920s, a group of Paducah businessmen recognized that an automobile bridge across the Ohio River was critical to the future development and prosperity of the community. A Paducah Board of Trade committee was established to promote construction of a bridge. After securing funding through state bonds, the bridge construction began in October, 1927. The ten spans of the bridge measured 4208 feet, the longest of which is on the Kentucky side and measures 715 feet. The bridge had a clearance of 53 feet above the 1913 high water mark. The cost of the bridge was $1,256,000.

The bridge was opened on May 8, 1929 with a giant parade, typical of Paducah. Ribbons were cut by the mayors of Paducah and Brookport and Hazel Miller of Paducah, who was named Miss Ohio. Then 1300 automobiles lined up behind the Tilghman and Washington schools bands and crossed over the bridge.

The foresight of these citizens was fortunate as America entered into the Depression period in October of that year. The opening of the Paducah-Brookport Bridge symbolically marked the end of a period of enormous prosperity and growth for Paducah.

AUTOMOBILE BRIDGE ACROSS OHIO RIVER, PADUCAH, KY.

THE SHORT CUT ROUTE CONNECTING FEDERAL HIGHWAYS, NORTH AND SOUTH   1324-29

1931–1950

While the nation as a whole faced lean times in the 1930s, Paducah was fortunate to have a solid base of businesses and manufacturers and the town's economy remained fairly stable through the Great Depression. Some locally owned firms did close in the early 1930s and the community responded by making special efforts to attract outside investments. In some cases, the city purchased vacant manufacturing sites and offered these to outside companies. The most important victims of the depression were several of Paducah's major financial institutions which failed, including the City National Bank and the First National Bank.

The major investment in the community and the surrounding area were made through government programs. The TVA dam on the Tennessee River provided both construction jobs and cheap power. The Kentucky Ordnance Works was located in western McCracken County during World War II to produce munitions. The favorable location of these government programs in western Kentucky was guided by the lobbying efforts of Alben Barkley, the Graves county native who rose to the top of American politics in the 1930s and 1940s.

Paducah endured its greatest challenge in 1937 when flood waters covered seven-eighths of the town and forced the evacuation of 27,000 people. After the flood, many citizens moved to new suburban neighborhoods in the elevated areas of the town. This shift in population was one of the 1937 Flood's greatest impacts. Another was the construction of the $6 million floodwall and levee system around the town to prevent any similar events.

The 1940s did see one amazing comeback — the return of the river industry. Diesel-powered boats were able to move millions of tons of cargo at extremely low costs and river transportation became the most economical way to move raw materials. Paducah again claimed the title "River City."

The Paducah Drive-In on Lone Oak Road (now demolished).

This cow remained on the second-story porch of a N. 6th Street house throughout the flood.

THE 1937 FLOOD

The 1937 Flood is probably the most important event in Paducah's history in the twentieth century. This devastating event can best be described in the statistics associated with it:

•During the month of January 1937, Kentucky, Indiana and Illinois experienced the heaviest rainfalls in their histories.

•In Paducah, the rainfall totals for the month of January reached 17.52 inches, half of the normal amount for an entire year. It rained 16 days straight that month.

•The Ohio River stage at Paducah was over 50 feet for over a month, with flood stage being at 43 feet. The flood reached its crest of 60.8 feet on February 3, 1937.

•Flood waters covered seven-eighths of the city, causing the evacuation of 27,000 people.

•Weather and flood conditions knocked out all electrical services in the city and prevented access to drinking water and food. Only 30 telephones in the western section of town operated during the flood.

•At the crest of the flood, over 2 million cubic feet of water flowed by Paducah ever second. An estimated 60 billion tons of water passed down the Ohio River during the flood period.

•Flood waters reached heights of 10 feet at the Market House and 8 feet at the Citizens Bank Building. The flood waters continued west to 28th Street before beginning to recede.

•Local carpenters built 200 johnboats in one day to help with the evacuation of citizens. Other boats were brought from the East Coast to help with the rescue of citizens from homes and businesses.

•The local Red Cross served 41,000 meals during the flood. Local citizens also pitched in to help, such as Captain Louis Igert who purchased the entire stock of two grocery stores and served 15,000 meals.

•The flood resulted in $12 million in damage to private homes, $6.5 million to retail establishments. Total losses amounted to $20 million.

•A stone memorial was erected at the point on Jefferson Street where the flood waters reached. This memorial was dedicated to all those who gave aid during the flood.

•A $6.2 million flood levee and wall system was constructed around Paducah to prevent future flooding.

Picturesque but devastating — icy fingers of winter clutching business lane. Paducah's Super-Flood. ©*Fred Neuman.*

Life-saving boats awaiting orders at dock on west Broadway. Paducah's Super-Flood. ©*Fred Neuman.*

COCA-COLA BOTTLING PLANT

One of America's favorite architectural styles for monumental buildings in the 1930s and 1940s was Art Deco. Typified by bold geometric forms and stylized decoration, the Art Deco style utilized modern building materials like colored glazed bricks, terra cotta, mosaic tiles, metal panels, glass bricks and carrerra glass.

Paducah's greatest Art Deco structure is the Coca-Cola Bottling Plant, located at the intersection of Broadway and LaBelle Street. Built by Luther Carson between 1937 and 1939, this plant replaced an older bottling plant on Sixth Street. The new plant, designed by Metropolis, Illinois architect Lester Daly, has an unusual hexagonal shape that follows the corner lot. Decorative concrete panels display the name of the plant and three-dimensional figures of Coke bottles. Rising from the top of the building is a copper dome where a fantastic light sequence flashes at night.

The interior of the building is as interesting as the exterior. In the central rotunda, the terrazzo tile floor is laid in a circular geometric pattern with the Coca-Cola logo in the center. A huge chandelier hangs from the center of the rotunda, which has plates of glass cut into the outline of a Coke bottle. The elegant stairway leading to the second floor offices has a solid nickel bronze railing. All of the office doors have been curved to follow the circular curve of the rotunda.

One of the most beautiful rooms in the building is Luther Carson's office, which has walls and a ceiling paneled in red gum and custom-made furniture. The entire building reflected his insistence on "nothing but the best."

Although the building is no longer used for bottling, the Coca-Cola Bottling Plant continues to fascinate new generations of Paducahans.

WORLD WAR II HOMEFRONT IN PADUCAH

Paducah proudly took part in the spirit of patriotism and sacrifice that swept across the country as America entered into World War II.

Local citizens were determined to do their part. Scrap drives were held to gather materials for the war effort. The Citizens Savings Bank participated by donating 1,200 pounds of iron bars from its front windows. Some people donated iron fences and gates from their front yards. Even the iron cannons from Lang Park were donated to the war effort.

Other citizens did their part by purchasing war bonds and stamps. Hollywood celebrities like Gene Tierney visited Paducah to promote the sale of these bonds.

Special performances were held at the Columbia Theater in order to sell "Invasion Bonds." Signs at the Citizens Savings Bank building urged people to "do your part" by joining the Civil Defense Corps. When the 1942 Strawberry Festival was canceled because of the war, local merchants held a "Victory Week" defense bonds and stamp sale instead.

The war effort did provide some much needed jobs locally. The headline for the March 3, 1942 edition of the *Paducah Sun-Democrat* announced that a $30 million arms plant was to be built in McCracken County. This plant took ten months to build and employed 6,000 construction workers and 1,200 production workers. The new plant, known as the Kentucky Ordnance Works, was another benefit to the region provided by the efforts of Alben Barkley.

Many local citizens participated in the military war effort. An airport was built in the county and used by the Army Air Force for the training of pilots. Paducah's highest ranking officer serving in the war was Joe Clifton, a decorated pilot and squadron leader who became a vice admiral.

BROADWAY FROM THIRD STREET, PADUCAH, KY.—22

Alben W. Barkley (signature)

Kentucky's most influential citizen in national politics in the twentieth century has been Alben Barkley. Born in a small farming community in Graves County, Barkley rose in the world of politics until he held the second most important position in the country — vice president of the United States.

Alben Barkley was born on November 24, 1877, in a log cabin in Wheel, Kentucky. He showed great talent at an early age and his parents made a special effort to encourage his education. After studying at Marvin College in Clinton, Kentucky, and Emory University in Atlanta, Georgia, Barkley came to Paducah where he read law under several local attorneys. He was admitted to the bar in 1901, married in 1903 and began building a substantial local legal practice.

Barkley's public service career began in 1905 when he was elected county attorney. He then rose in the world of politics to McCracken County Judge Executive, U. S. Congressman and United States Senator. His skill and dedication in the U. S. Senate allowed him to be elected majority leader. His prominence in the Democratic Party led him to be chosen as the keynote speaker for three national conventions. At the 1948 convention, his keynote speech was so powerful that he was chosen as the vice presidential candidate to run with Harry Truman. Elected in an upset, Barkley and Truman proved to be a good partnership as they led the country between 1949 and 1953.

Alben Barkley died in 1956 following a speech at Washington and Lee University. His final words: "I would rather be a servant in the house of the Lord than sit in the seats of the Mighty."

Harry Truman and Alben Barkley at the 1948 National Democratic Convention.

"Angles", Home of Vice-President Alben W. Barkley, Paducah, Kentucky

PHOTO BY DR. RAYMOND L. ROOF

ALBEN W. BARKLEY
1877 - 1956
"I would rather be a servant in
the house of the Lord than to
sit in the seats of the mighty"

SPONSORED BY
PADUCAH JUNIOR CHAMBER OF COMMERCE
KENTUCKY STATE FEDERATION OF LABOR

Alben Barkley memorial erected on Jefferson Street.

1951–1970

After years of sluggish local economic conditions, Paducah was transformed dramatically in 1951 when the Atomic Energy Commission announced that it would build a billion dollar atomic enrichment plant in McCracken County. A "boom" followed as 20,000 workers moved to town to work on the construction site for the atomic energy plant and other associated facilities, such as the Shawnee Steam Plant.

The location of the plant and many other regional economic development projects can be attributed to the sponsorship of Alben Barkley, vice president of the United States under Harry Truman. The western Kentucky region continues to enjoy the many benefits and projects connected to Alben Barkley's influence.

In the years following the construction of the atomic energy facility, commonly known as the Carbide plant, it continued to be the area's largest employer. Local economic prosperity was also promoted by the continued expansion of the local river industry, especially the growth of barge lines that specialized in the transportation of raw materials. Another prominent local employer, the Illinois Central railroad shops, began to employ fewer people as the railroad moved from steam to diesel-powered locomotives.

Several important local traditions began in the 1950s and 1960s. The Lions Club-WPSD telethon began in 1957 to raise money for the Easter Seal Centers. The Summer Festival, kicked off in 1967, was a summertime celebration on the riverfront and in downtown Paducah. The annual Dogwood Festival began to highlight the spring blooming season in Paducah and the night time Lighted Dogwood Trail became a popular tradition.

The community began to restore and redevelop its historic buildings, beginning with the Market House in the 1960s. This restoration effort was accompanied by the construction of one of Paducah's most prominent buildings, the City Hall.

ATOMIC ENERGY COMMISSION PLANT — UNION CARBIDE

On December 14, 1950, the *Paducah Sun-Democrat* headline revealed "Billion Dollar Atomic Plant for Paducah." After months of rumor and speculation, the Atomic Energy Commission announced that it was building a gaseous diffusion plant for uranium enrichment in Paducah.

The AEC was attracted to Paducah because of such factors as plentiful water, well-developed transportation systems, inexpensive TVA power and access to fuel from regional coal mines. The lobbying efforts of then Vice President Alben Barkley also must have played a major role in the plant site selection.

Work on the plant started in 1951. The $500 million project occupied 7,335 acres, including the former site of the Kentucky Ordnance Works. The construction project transformed Paducah. Over 20,000 workers came to town to work on the plant's construction and at the nearby power plants that were also being constructed. The population of Paducah almost doubled in two years, creating critical situations in the areas of housing, traffic control, recreational opportunities, education and medical care. Typical of the plant's impact on the area — five new drive-ins were built to handle the demand for something to do on the weekend.

Work on the plant was completed in 1956. The plant became Paducah and McCracken County's largest employer and its existence has assured continued growth and prosperity for the community.

CENTENNIAL CELEBRATION

Local gentlemen started growing beards and ladies pulled out antique dresses and bonnets as a special Centennial Celebration was held in 1956 to mark the 100th anniversary of Paducah's incorporation as a city.

The highlight of the yearlong celebration was the Centennial Week that was held from July 30th to August 4th. The week started with a three-mile parade down Broadway which featured 70 floats, antique automobiles, marching bands, steam calliopes, buggies and wagons. Another event included a torch parade honoring the Centennial queen and her court followed by a fireworks display on the riverfront. Other days included a car and boat show on the riverfront and a Governor's Day honoring the governors of Kentucky, Tennessee, and Illinois. Local history was highlighted at a centennial pageant, the Saga of Paducah, that was put on at Keiler Field for a week and included over 500 participants.

During the celebration, local men were encouraged to grow beards and over 1,000 registered to be in the beard-judging competition. The world's largest pie, a six-foot peach pie, was created and offered to the public for consumption. The *Paducah Sun-Democrat* produced ten special Centennial editions that featured special historic topics, like riverboat days and the history of the Paducah city government.

While Paducah was celebrating its history, a controversy developed concerning one of the town's most beloved landmarks. A petition was circulated by the local Association of Commerce calling for the demolition of the Market House for a parking lot. The opposition to this proposal was immediate and strong. Led by Mrs. Sara Smith Campbell and the local chapter of the Daughters of the American Revolution, opponents were able to convince the city government to preserve the building. As a safeguard to its future preservation, a bronze plaque was attached to the Market House honoring William Clark and the building was dedicated as a historic shrine.

All decked out for the Centennial Celebration: from left, Miss Dorothy Wiemann, Mrs. Emmett Knight, and Miss Jeanette Broyles.

FILMING OF "HOW THE WEST WAS WON"

The banks of the Ohio and Cumberland rivers returned to an earlier era when parts of the movie *How the West Was Won* were filmed around Smithland, Kentucky, and Battery Rock, Illinois. Featuring such stars as James Stewart, Carroll Baker and Debbie Reynolds, the movie was filmed in Cinerama and directed by veterans Henry Hathaway and John Ford. The portion of the movie filmed around Paducah dealt with the passage of a pioneer family down the Ohio River on its way west. Scenes included the family fighting with river pirates and trying to survive when their raft was caught in rapids. The producers' desire for authentic-

Director Henry Hathaway (left) and actor James Stewart (center).

ity included converting a derelict boat into a stern-wheeler steamboat for a scene of Civil War soldiers returning from the war, and constructing a farm setting, complete with weathered cabin, barn and family graveyard, at the juncture of the Ohio and Cumberland rivers. The actual filming of scenes along the Ohio River required the stationing of a highway patrolman several miles upstream with a walkie-talkie to warn of approaching boats. All filming had to cease until the boats passed.

Actors Andy Devine (in carriage) and George Peppard perform in front of the CINERAMA camera and the MGM crew.

NEW CITY HALL

Representative of Paducah's progressive spirit in the 1960s was the decision to build a new city hall. Its construction in 1965 was part of an urban renewal project that created a fountain plaza and complex of governmental buildings on the south side of the downtown area.

The City of Paducah hired internationally-known architect Edward Durell Stone to design the new governmental center. Stone was a leading exponent of modern classicism. The Paducah City Hall is a good example of this style, which combines balanced classical design with a modern functional usage.

The Paducah City Hall sits on a broad concrete base in the middle of an entire block. Two-story concrete columns create colonnades on all four sides of the building. The central atrium is topped with a pyramidal lantern that lets light into the interior of the building.

What is fascinating about the Paducah City Hall is that it has a "twin" in New Delhi, India. Edward Durell Stone also designed the American Embassy Building in India, which is an almost exact duplicate of the Paducah structure.

There is one physical reminder in the 1965 City Hall of the 1882 City Hall that it replaced. Displayed in the entryway is the bronze bell that once rang the time from the tower of the old city hall. This bell has been restored and placed on display as a reminder of Paducah's heritage.

City Hall, Paducah, Kentucky

RESTORATION OF THE MARKET HOUSE

Paducah's isolation from major cities has allowed the community to develop its own exciting and diverse arts programming.

The successful effort to save the historic Market House in the 1960s provided a home to three important local arts organizations. The Paducah Art Guild was originally organized in 1957 in the Carnegie Library and held one of its first exhibits by hanging artwork on the flood wall. The founder of Paducah Art Guild was Miss Mary Yeiser, an art instructor at Paducah Junior College and one of the community's most respected artists. In the 1960s, the Paducah Art Guild took over the north end of the Market House and developed its gallery space there.

In that same period, a community theater group known as the Market House Theater occupied the south end of the building. Starting with a simple stage and folding chairs, the theater has grown to a modern, 250-seat facility where ten to twelve mainstage productions are performed each year.

The center section of the Market House has been developed as the William Clark Market House Museum. This facility contains such historic artifacts as the first mechanized fire truck in Paducah and a 800 pound bell from a river packet boat. The centerpiece of the museum is the ornate gingerbread interior from the Robertson-DuBois Drug Store (later known as List Drug Store) that was reinstalled in the Market House. The museum also contains exhibits on Paducah's two most famous citizens, Alben Barkley and Irvin Cobb.

Interior of the Market House Museum. Photo courtesy of the Paducah Tourist Commission.

PADUCAH MARINE WAYS

The Paducah Marine Ways celebrated its 125th year of operations in 1970. Since 1845, this facility had continued to repair and build boats for the inland waterways system.

The ownership of Paducah Marine Ways had passed through several hands since the original owners, the Watts-Given Company. The facility was purchased in 1945 by the St. Louis Shipbuilding Company. That year, the wooden railways running into the Ohio River were removed and replaced with modern ties. The facility began a barge-building program as part of the growing demand for use of the rivers as a means to transport huge amounts of raw materials with diesel-powered tugboats and barges.

By 1970, employment at the facility had grown to 300 people and annual sales were $5.5 million. The marine ways at Paducah was the largest shipyard in Kentucky. It was capable of new construction as well as repair of barges and in 1970 was building open hopper barges and petroleum-transporting barges.

Paducah Marine Ways remained in operation until the 1980s. The closing of this facility ended an important chapter in Paducah's history that closely paralleled the development of the community.

INDUSTRY IN
PADUCAH, KY.

MAGNAVOX OF KENTUCKY
RADIOS

PADUCAH MARINE WAYS
BOAT BUILDING & REPAIRS

ILLINOIS CENTRAL RAILROAD SHOPS
LOCOMOTIVE REBUILDING AND REPAIRING

WALTER G. HOUGLAND SONS, Inc.
RIVER TRANSPORTATION

CLAUSSNER HOSIERY CO.
HOSIERY

MODINE MANUFACTURING CO.
RADIATORS
2C-H988

1971–PRESENT

From 1971 to the present, Paducah has continued in its role as a regional center in the retail, education, financial, medical, entertainment and arts areas.

Several Paducah institutions enjoyed impressive growth during this period. Paducah Community College, which had moved to its Blandville Road campus in 1964 and had merged with the University of Kentucky in 1968, continued to expand its educational components and add to its enrollment. The three local banking institutions either built new head-quarters or refurbished their existing buildings. The local art community expanded, with the continued success of the Market House Theatre and the Paducah Art Guild and the creation of the Paducah Symphony Orchestra. A new Lourdes Hospital was built and Western Baptist Hospital expanded as Paducah grew as a medical community.

Efforts to beautify and revitalize downtown Paducah began. The Townlift Project in 1978 sponsored beautification efforts along Broadway and around the Market House. Important revitalization projects include the restoration of such landmarks as the Irvin Cobb Hotel, Citizens Bank Building, Old Peoples Bank Building, Cohen Building, Elks Lodge, Sinnott Hotel, Grace Episcopal Church, St. Francis de Sales Catholic Church and the Winstead Drug Store.

A symbol for this period of revitalization was the restoration of the derelict James P. Smith Family House as the Whitehaven Tourist Welcome Center, the only historic house in America that has been restored as an interstate welcome center.

Paducah gained special distinction for being "Quilt City USA" with the establishment of the American Quilter's Society show in 1985 and the construction of the Museum of the American Quilter's Society in 1991.

Paducah Ambassadors and the Delta Queen.

HISTORIC RESTORATION EFFORTS

In the late 1970s, downtown Paducah started a period of revitalization with the Townlift Project. This beautification project focused on Broadway and the Market House Square area and included the removal of all overhead wiring, placement of utilities under the ground, and the creation of a new streetscape with brick sidewalks, planters, benches and new light poles and traffic signals. Downtown merchants removed protruding signs and repainted historic storefronts to highlight architectural details. Flowering trees and shrubs were planted along the streets creating a greenway in downtown Paducah in spring and summer.

A major downtown restoration project took place in 1979 when the Hotel Irvin Cobb was converted into housing for senior citizens. This important project not only saved a beloved local landmark but brought people back downtown to live.

The George Wallace House in 1894.

Other innovative restoration projects followed. The old Peoples Bank Building was adapted as law offices and the significant interior features, such as the brass and marble teller cages, were retained in the restoration. The redevelopment of the Citizens Bank Building was a successful combination of the restoration of a historic building with the construction of a modern addition. The Cohen Building project allowed the restoration of one of downtown Paducah's best cast-iron storefronts as well as the building's Italianate detailing.

The preservation effort also spread to the historic Lower Town neighborhood as Italianate, Queen Anne, Romanesque and Classical Revival houses were purchased and restored. Since 1980, this effort has been led by the Lower Town Neighborhood Association.

Ninth Street House in the Lower Town neighborhood.

WHITEHAVEN TOURIST WELCOME CENTER

During the 1970s, the local community watched with alarm and regret the gradual decline of the beautiful James P. Smith House on Lone Oak Road. Prominently situated near Interstate 24, the white Classical Revival house with its Corinthian-columned front portico fascinated both local citizens and travelers passing through Kentucky.

The house itself is Paducah's finest residential example of the Classical Revival style. The two-story brick house was built in the 1860s by Edward Anderson and remodeled in 1903 by owner Ed L. Atkins and his architect A. L. Lassiter. The house was purchased in 1907 for $7,000 by James P. Smith and it remained in the Smith family until 1981.

In the 1970s, the house was no longer lived in and it quickly deteriorated due to vandalism and water damage. It appeared destined for demolition until May of 1981 when the state of Kentucky expressed interest in purchasing the house and restoring it for an interstate tourist welcome center. Restoration work began in June 1982 and the house opened to the public in 1983. The site was named the Whitehaven Tourist Welcome Center in a revival of an early name for the house. Whitehaven is the only historic house in America that has been restored as an interstate tourist welcome center. It was listed on the National Register of Historic Places in 1984.

The welcome center is now open 24 hours a day for travelers on Interstate 24. The historic rooms of the house have been decorated with

Smith House in 1981.

period furnishings and tours are given daily. A display of memorabilia connected to Alben Barkley's life is also seen on the tour.

Because of its beauty and significance, Whitehaven stands as a proud symbol of this community.

Whitehaven Tourist Welcome Center.

RIVERFRONT-DOWNTOWN
IMPROVEMENT PROJECT

Throughout the 1980s, the citizens of Paducah continued to discover the importance of the town's riverfront area. In the late 1980s, community and governmental leaders worked intensively to create a master plan for the development of the riverfront area. Outside experts who visited Paducah reminded the community that the riverfront was one of the town's greatest resources. Under the leadership of Mayor Gerry Montgomery, a blueprint for the future redevelopment of the riverfront was created.

Plans for the redevelopment of the riverfront area received a giant boost in 1990 when Governor Wallace Wilkinson and the Kentucky General Assembly appropriated $5 million for the project. The overall project components included the following:

•conversion of a lot at 2nd and Broadway into a concrete-surfaced, tree-lined parking lot;

•creation of a mini-park at the corner of 2nd and Broadway that contains a gazebo, carriage drive, benches and information directory. The park has been paved with bricks inscribed with names of donors, a project that has been sponsored by Paducah Main Street, Inc.;

•development of a Second Street Promenade from the Market House to the Executive Inn that includes brick walkways lined with trees, benches and gaslight-period lighting;

•creation of a floodwall opening between Broadway and Jefferson that allows an expanded view of the river. State-of-the-art floodgates have been designed for this opening;

•construction of a passenger terminal on the riverfront to serve as a mooring place for excursion boats such as the Mississippi Queen and the Delta Queen;

•placement of new or upgraded utility lines in the riverfront area to accommodate future development.

Photo courtesy of the Paducah Tourist Commission.

INFORMATION AGE PARK

On September 18, 1991, the Greater Paducah Economic Development Council announced that the new Paducah Information Age Park was to be constructed in the western section of McCracken County. This complex was defined as an office park for businesses and corporations using telecommunications and computers to provide marketing and other services for the business world. The project was hailed by local and state leaders as a key to future economic prosperity and growth in Paducah and McCracken County. Officials estimated that 2,500 to 7,500 new jobs could be created within 10 years.

A local investment of $5 million was expected to have a return of $100 to $300 million in private investment. The initial investment allowed the purchase of a 600 acre parcel of land in McCracken County, the building of a resource center, the paving of roads for site improvements, and to extend fiber optics to the site. The resource center was described as the key element to the project. It contains a teleconference center, interactive classrooms, a child care center, office space and conference rooms.

A critical factor in the development of the Info Park has been Bell South's commitment to the project. The company pledged $2 million to extending critical telecommunication services to the park. Bell South also pledged marketing assistance to identify and recruit tenants to the park.

On the day of the announcement of the info park, many local leaders commented that this economic development was probably the most dramatic announcement to come to the community since the early 1950s when Paducah was chosen as the site for the government's gaseous diffusion plant.

MASTER LANDSCAPE PLAN :
RESOURCE CENTER PERSPECTIVE PADUCAH INFORMATION AGE PARK PADUCAH KY

"QUILT CITY USA"

Paducah has gained the title "Quilt City USA" since it has become the home of the American Quilter's Society and its museum and annual show.

The AQS was founded in 1984 by Bill and Meredith Schroeder, who put on the society's first quilt show and contest in 1985. The AQS now has the largest quilt show in the country, with cash prizes totaling more than $75,000. Participants from all over the world attend the quilt show in Paducah each year where over 400 contemporary quilts and wall hangings are displayed. Fashion shows, lectures, seminars and workshops make up an important part of this event.

In 1991, the Museum of the American Quilter's Society opened. This 30,000 square foot facility has three climate-controlled galleries, plus classrooms, a gift shop, a conference room and a reference room. The museum features a rotating selection from the museum's permanent collection of quilts purchased at the annual show and from other sources. The museum also features special historical, contemporary, thematic and regional exhibits of quilts. Workshops and seminars on quilting are also presented throughout the year at the museum.

Paducah holds a Dogwood Festival each spring that is enjoyed by the more than 30,000 visitors to the quilt show. Special art exhibits, theatrical performances and displays of antique quilts are planned. Downtown merchants decorate storefront windows with quilt displays. The entire community extends a special sense of hospitality as Paducah celebrates being "Quilt City USA."